SONGS OF
THE BLOOD

KATE MACALISTER

songs of the blood

QUERENCIA

Querencia Press, LLC
Chicago Illinois

QUERENCIA PRESS

LIBRARY OF CONGRESS CATALOG-IN-PUBLICATION DATA

ISBN 979 8 9860788 4 7

www.querenciapress.com

First Published in 2022

Querencia Press, LLC
Chicago IL

Printed & Bound in the United States of America

CONTENTS

These words are dedicated to all Social Justice Witches and their alley cats.

FOREWORD by Chloe Hanks

In *Songs of the Blood*, Kate MacAlister makes a defiant debut as a powerfully lyrical poet. Her words are illustrative, and oftentimes conversational, taking the reader by the hand and leading them into a daydream. MacAlister's poetry is musical, as though each word dances with the blank space to create a fearless spectacle that leaves the reader spellbound. We begin with 'Submission.' MacAlister entices us with magic, and urges her reader into silence, giving us a moment to hear her and feel the power of her words. With poems that recall falling in love, being haunted by a lover, even captivated by a lover— readers can find comfort and familiarity in falling under the spell. As she moves us along, the poems gain a life of their own. As we are drawn into 'Devotion,' we become lost in the melody of the poetry. We are drawn into the conversation, offered a perspective beyond the words on the page. By the time MacAlister has guided us into 'Rebellion,' we are at her disposal. Her poetry is precise, powerful and urgent; the voice of the Witch erupts through the music, bringing the rebellion to life.

There is something folkloric and at times seductive on the pages of this book. Each moment in the journey feels weighted and symbolic. There is a nostalgia in the concept and a familiarity in the story; but something about MacAlister's work makes the Witch feel renewed. Living beyond her legacy, she is dancing on the pages with us. A stunning debut from an elegant poet that begs to be read and revisited, *Songs of the Blood* will sit magically among company on your poetry shelf.

-Chloe Hanks author of *I Call Upon the Witches*
May 2022

I
SUBMISSION

Cardiac Arrest

small words between your teeth
books for a love
unwritten

the terms of my surrender
chiseled
on my ribcage

the dawn sets fire to the curtains
I fall
wondering
under what sky will
I be cracking open
my chest for you

spelling out unspeakable truths
while you forage through treasures
rare
cursed and
forgotten

those
pages once
scrawled in red ink
drawn from veins
close to the spirit
about all these
lost boys

rendered
unsung
in the wake
of your silent

light

my blood is a lucid confession
to you
worshipping

a flawless mask
of an open heart

Séance

I dream
your bones creak
with the night

your body
marked
still
wounded
adorned with the runes
of my touch

A sacrifice
to the
Deep Blue
begging for land
as you move
with the waves

I am restless
at the bottom
of our ocean

listening to
the hymns
of your wide
eyes
and
gasping
breaths

Delilah smoking on the front door step at dawn

I trap you
snared
into my full-blooded tresses
on a Friday night
(just in case there is nothing left to say)
washed out
on a Monday morning eclipse
I feel my comforts are running out
a distant tremor rippled through your hands
in my mouth
all hard palate and soft sails set
on spiked waves of axonial potential
gentle light-taming agent provocateurs
of songs
delving into
thick skinned honey fruit
ordinary devotions
to an incurable disease
just another
liaison
a mundane sacrifice
sprawled divinely
across
the morning altar

chiaroscuro

you crown me
a cheap queen
beneath your garden window
and in charming cafes
         (with you la vie est belle—just means c'est la vie)
mostly after dark
or just before the dawn
it must be a trick of the light

your scars
become invisible
in the hours of
night-time hunger
when you are almost
   but never
mine

Love Songs
on the tip of each word
your fear clasped
so tight
across my lips
I let myself drown in
sugar-coated suffocation
washing over me
hearing you
speak in divine tongues
for seven satanical hours

tales drifting in and out of dreams
1 AM and the
witching hour passes almost unnoticed
when you mumble something about

a High Priestess
and an Empress
drinking from the same cup

I froze on the silver lining
hymnal
anew
and
again

Lion Court

I stalk
black alley cats
and
white rabbits

a scarlet veil
of
lace and lies
sows your magic

familiar spell casting
on the avenues
of a wandering city
 —your hunting ground
asleep

I find myself
blinded
in your garden
all this talk of
magnolia and cherry blossom
draped carelessly upon me

silken copper spills
over the silver moon
like a crooked smile
the birds of the night
feverishly scream
echoing
your songs
in my soul
these Bedroom Hymns
roar through

all my pretty ornaments
make all my
bones shake
and
your bravest blood
echoes through this ghost town
painted red

offer up
that beating heart
of yours
in your hours of
desperate
sin

January Tea - Ginger

in a perfectly measured box
I lay with Bluebeard's girls
the last one still warm
her lacy black pants
dangling from the end of the bed
barely wide enough for two

and as you blush
I start to dream
of the tales
laying here
all your lost muses
maybe once sisters
singing with the seagulls
in the wild void
of your marks and stitches

"that'll only take 2 weeks to heal"
(what an awfully long time for just a scratch)

love looked better
when it was more than
just a little bit
I listen deeply
dying breaths
and
nothing left to say

Exhale
Kiss
Break me

Open

actually, IGAF

all the men I ever loved lived on this street
with the wolves and cherry blossoms // the coffee and
gasoline the blood and the laughter //
the seagull songs and the humid days // the bare feet on
cobblestone
my hair thickened after the rain // after you
I braid it just after dawn
sitting up in your shrine for an age lost
silk frayed to ginger threads // what a signature look for
selling you another moon
adrift in your twilight for these 3 or 4 years // withered
but I always feel the dying world through
your skin // on mine
> *(I let you break me all night*
> *:but god does it feel good:*
> *god does it make me feel alive)*
your silence is sacred
in the dark // in the light
of days to come // it's probably indifference making me
scream //
fuck you
Deep
while the blood still runs
Wild

Comrades

I lay my eyes down on the meadow
of the crescent moon
rising on your thigh
behind the wheat or the barley
is no trace of the wind
only the blade a flicker in the

Dark

it should be on the left
but this is
just so right

 what if
   what if
      what if

our words run dry
and I am left
once again on the
hourglass shore
gasping for air
swallowing
all this sand in
the aftermath of
a storm
a scythe
reaping
in my dilated heart
entwined in cotton sheets
you tell me again and again
you know the way
out of the woods and

into the wild
where my voice is fed
raised on jasmine
and foxglove

you're right
I am feral

and
these kisses
are out for revenge
an eye for a tooth
an eye tooth for silver lashes

eviscerating every
atom of him
I barely sense
in the grove of
your surface skin

evening prayers
sequestered
Blue and Purple
bloom in my veins
and along porcelain legs

your words
marking me

we've all been eaten alive
one time or another

seen // unsent

it split my lip //   *I will always be a little bit in love*
with you...too
just a little bit // more and we would witness the shadows
of
some sort of situation alienated // a surplus fairytale of a
couple of normative years

I can't help but wonder // when you sealed this tomb of
worship
crinkled sheets and burnt coffee and the lies // piles of *I am*
still reading that
what spells of mine // would you leave behind

in the wooden drawer // right next to
where you slept // where I screamed
all those nights // when the last small death
drawn together // becomes an omen

   Let's be strangers once again

for there is no rest for the wicked
women // those crazy bitches never sleep //
for a lot can happen in one night // and the light of the first
cherry dawn
sailing on the horizon whispers // of your days in the sun
I can steer this ship // I have seen rougher waters // and
lived

your light falling through my cracks // was an ocean
burning

II
DEVOTION

POV: she wears layers for fall

coffee past eleven
Will you stay the night?
   —*Can we play hide and seek?*
Maybe only the "hide" part, my love.
   —*Because lately it's all just seek and destroy?*
and although I am safe in the fort between your breaths
nothing here can cushion these blows

   —*I keep telling you.*
   I don't talk. You know?

but in this moment
dancing in the cathedral
your name drips
of my bitten lip
like caramel syrup
~the taste of an eclipse
tonight

 I will wear it to the bone
smear it all over my teeth
like crushed cinnamon lipstick
bleeding into the dawn

until my tongue comes undone
and sure, I would love him
but would he taste
like your mouth
in the dark
before sunrise

songs of the blood

in a twilight room
on a Tuesday afternoon
I meet her again
on a level that hasn't broken
yet
we
come
together
witness a new goddess

what she calls grains of life
I named a storm

tasting her songs
I feel the starlight in my bones
and hear the trees whisper to me

'Save us
  Save us
    Save us
       now'

her roots wrapped gently around
each vessel

between burning
and drowning
and love
(did no one tell her?)
the heart is a muscle that splinters

bathing in the river
laying within the words

of all these women calling

lingering
linking hands
unbraiding her gold
she laughs
~just imagine
being loved by
m e n

camera obscura

a tarot princess
on my pillow
then a wannabe sorceress
kneeling at the end
of a brass bed

worshipping
your temple
your flesh

in cheap red wine
in black and white

all the years of longing
unmarked
crashed and burned
(my sweet heart)
between the ribs

spilled milk tea brewed
with
dusky cinnamon
and
dragon ~~fruit~~ flesh

I graze on your
Homecoming
until we find
the map through the ghost town
        the grey
            sticky
              silence

it's a trespasser's wickerwork
a secret woven in the light
of your scars
some hardened
some fresh
with soft blood

leading
our coven
back into the fire

Sea Serpents

born beneath
fading sky
the once priceless curtain falls
devouringly drowning
my entangled hair

when
your steps mumble
a promise to
this path

shrieking with
the silence of darkened nights
and
sighing with
the weight of the universe
undone
the mouth full of leaves of the past summer

I lay still among
the reeds
beholding the battle
the agony
screaming
in your pleading breast

your infinity is
gold-plated evanescence
—conquered beneath me
when
this wilderness
throbs trembling

each breath
so heavy
every heartbeat
taking flight

~before the morning draws
close

indomitable
the waves intoxicate
the song of this midsummer night

and in the last resounding cry of doom
I begin to understand;

in your eyes stars are born

Ghost Books

it wasn't you
but the ocean
calling
dancing on
your hallowed ground
so late
making it rain daylight
for you
before the dawn

still that
voice
rumbled as
mountains
under siege
vibrating in
every osteoclast
caught up
in the stardust
making up

me

undone
when you told me
to come home
and I forgot
how to lead
the way

beneath Boneyard Creek

prairie honey
still stuck in
the rifts
flooded with
golden lights
of fireflies
dying in quince summer nights
singing the bones

a silver lining climbs
my spinal cord like
an oak
when those
stars fell out
of your mouth
in the rain
on the porch

and all of me
a northern star
washed with
wildfires of
the golden coast
ebbs into your
breathless lullaby

setting aside
Christmas morning creaks
for handwritten
letters on
the wall

Equinox

nights in your eyes
frosted glances
enriched with golden colours,
a delicate
feral substance

within the songs
of my
surrender
the avenues
blossomed

beneath
our feet
~the sleeping concrete

above
the dreaming stars of
an untamed summer

and your voice
was gently entwined
with the shadow
of my silent tears

all our fears
only
dancing whispers
on a glowing horizon
the backyards of the city
nothing but
opulent palaces of our thoughts

as dawn
broke
your windows

we bathed
delightfully
in the morning flames
our wings tired
and tenderly seared

the last starbreeze
fallen and vanquished
these disfigured hours of yesterday and now
a precious keepsake

tangled in
the Beauty of
lost Time
and the heartbeat
of your world
echoing heavily
within my
laughter

Exhale

formless forgiveness
casts shadows on
lost desire

a wistful voice
sings from deep within the woods
writes stories
of a summer night
on fragile strings

my solitude
~a dream inwrought with endlessness
my broken smile
blossoms on the surface of the memory

insignificantly
our cities burn
in twilight
and
stars gradually dissolve

      Shall we dance once more in their fading light?

remembering
every Death
between
you and me

I tremble
beneath the sacrificial altar
of your touch

the fall from paradise lost

—inspiring
—exquisite pain

volatile cracks
in my soul

break the silence

III
REBELLION

Hecate

There are three rules
written all over
the faces of witches

I.
women are water
we will do the breathing in
the dead space between
supposed to
and becoming
an ancient name
on each bloodied lip bitten
the salt in our wounds
growing pains

II.
women are soil
when the quickening comes
warbling of our blood
two streams thundering in the dark

(mothering the maidens in the garden)
we tame the fire
taking back the night
our songs
our streets
when we proclaim
"I like to burn"
owning each flame
the hearth unchained

III.
women are blood
bodies broken
break out the silence
a soul seen fighting calling to each scar
and hands working
pulling at the roots eaten away inside
unhinging this system
as if we had a choice

not all men

I dig for shelter
in a homespun endometrial layer
each new moon like the first rain
each crimson drop
seething in the
songs of
the blood
I mark myself
with the war paint
you made to keep me small
for my sisters
are coming
Home
thighs full of thunder
on shaking ground
Home
to
the night
the streets
the bargaining table
never yours to take
never yours to keep
we reclaim each of our stars
*(a raging red crown
of conquest)*
and despite it all
they still shine for
You

Siren Songs

a lullaby
gifted to the
the Deep Blue
feels more like that bruise
buried in my chest
rebel kings would never
crown me their queen

so I run
alongside my feral sisters howling
clawing
scratching
the glass ceilings
painting towns and grand palaces red

as our voices unfold stronger
wilder
with every lost cause
new moons
turn the crimson to blush
our war cries of forgotten sacrilege
kiss a new dawn
the rain of rebellion
trickling down our
bent
twisted
spines

change is coming tonight
I sense it
in the corner of
her smile
burning like gold

they don't burn witches anymore

no, they don't burn witches anymore
they blame victims
shame sluts
catcalls
a familiar
always by my side
one step ahead
or the steps heavy on
the pavement behind me
at night
when the keys cut my skin
and I call upon my sisters
knowing they cannot save
me
      this time

they don't burn witches anymore
since our grimoires
are
a collection of battle wounds
between my legs
and on my throat
when we told you again and again
      or just couldn't say
No
(*no*)
No

they don't burn witches anymore
the tell tale sign
the devil's mark
lingers in
my voice
when I summon

our spirits
to gather
when you sentence our mother
to the stake
poisoning our waters
making our bodies
prisons of flesh
as if it was written in the stars

they don't fear witches anymore
but their buildings shake
and hands tremble
when they point their fattened fingers
    "What a fucking bitch"
              (Witch)
it is not a curse
declining this deal of indulgences
I know why
I know why

they don't burn witches anymore
for
we are already
set on fire

Sanctuary

Cassandra's Tale
is lawlessly rewritten in colourless ink
when the flood comes
reach down
into the glistening
aorta
rooted
   (each beat slithering
               slipping
                        pushing clay through muddied
capillaries)

Dark
and
Deep
and
so
Cold
rising

you hold your breath
none the wiser
—sometimes we call this dying-

it's a matter of time
the shadow of a man
or two thinking
  *"I would rather serve
  than be salvaged"*
dreaming of the endless
voice of the Waters
setting broken hands

and eyes apart

staring in gaping wonder
did she speak truth
or curses
to power?

nothing will make you
listen
like a landslide beneath your feet

on
the ground you
kissed and blessed
Home

Crowd Control

a voice is out on the streets
the ghost
of urgency
calling to arms
and souls

a
forgotten art of
starting a fire
to steal the orderly show
of batons
and hollow money
talks

shattered glass
does not cloud the
caving eyes of dreamers
and lovers
burning
unravelling
Blood Red
or Grey
beyond white fences
and beautiful days

walking blind
your hand in mine
the concrete aching
sighing
with the weight
of a world
almost lost
almost won

my hand grasping theirs
I roar
for change
until we
all get there

two heartbeats in a
flutter of a thousand wings
tracing through

the screams
the pain
and
the dark

today
we breathe again

Sugar Maker Moon

this storm
we are brewing
rituals in coffee cups
a drop of rage
a drop of laughter
so wild
will pull out some
of the old man's
teeth
sweeping away
root
rot
nerves and
all
that was sacred

bodies we take to the streets

I will not
give my love
the names of the oppressors

a baptism of fierce fires
each nom de guerre
picked from the fuming asphalt
like paving stones

these first degree burns
sticky on our lips make it hard
to whisper
    so scream
blaze the trails
for the hearse
  where the heart of the beast lies
on broken glass and red satin

we will cauterize a wound
bleeding for generations
and
I will not define an embrace
by the chains and walls
twisting us in knots

when in your eyes
freedom calls

13 Coven

our words always trapped in
in our mothers' tongue
our fathers' words (hard to swallow)
grown
up and out
in a language
that calls a kick in the teeth
a kiss
tangled into a sentence of another time
another body ruling mine

these monsters in our heads
intrusive but harm-
less
compared to those
loose on the street
the dinner table
those holding our hands
in satin sheets
in law and order
dividing us by our suffering
this Beast
the Legion
praising our instinct for restoration

      (can't you see the storm in my eyes?)

my sisters gathered all of me here
(jin - jiyan - azadi - it means women, life and   freedom)
   if you scream loud enough

we will turn everything around
the inside out

starting with you
starting with me
partisans bowing at the altar
of feminine urges unbuttoned
these
b i t c h e s
are free

Inhale
...
Exhale

this is resistance.
catching our breath
giving life to laments
turned into hymns
of wars in the cradle
and the kitchen sink
for all the nights
stolen
for all our sisters
stolen
screaming

Death is a liar
and her hand on my heart
the tears in her dark eyes
beg
not. one. more.

but how? her ask quivers through
a city flooded and burnt
        women, first of all, need to be streetwise
don't submit

to arrest

oh no.
we shall burn it all down
rooting for
justice and peace
in the ashes
sown from the concrete jungle
to the prairie and back once again
we are keepers of the sacred
medullar grounds
bleeding out with love
to get it
out of
the system

we own flames too

Note on Previous Publications

Hecate, POV : she wears layers for fall, actually, IGAF - *"Depression is what killed the dinosaurs" anthology, Sunday Mornings at the River March 2022*
They don't burn witches, Siren Songs, Exhale, not all men - *For Women Who Roar & Voices of Rebellion zine*
not all men - *The Write Launch*
Crowd Control - *she speaks Anthology, Tipping the scales*
songs of the blood - *Meet me on Lesbos zine, sapphic writers*
camera obscura - *Free Verse Revolution Hades*
seen/unsent - *Gypsophilia Magazine*
January Tea – Ginger - *From Whispers to Roars*
Chiaroscuro - *Wingless Dreamer Competition - it's midnight*

About the Author

*"When we share our stories, we realize that we
are not alone with it. We begin to see the system that
behind violence, injustice and exploitation.
Telling our story is the connecting moment to take action
and to initiate change."*

Kate is an author, feminist activist and founder of the
multilingual community arts and literature project *Stimmen
der Rebellion/Dengê Berxwedane/Voices of Rebellion*.

Her works have been published in journals and anthologies
all over the world. Her poems are stories of human
connection and the dreams of revolution.

Coffee, her cat Bella, the occasional romantic disaster and,
naturally, her feminist friends are particularly important
for her creative process.

Find Kate on Instagram at
@kissed.by_fire.

9 798986 078847